# MUSIC MAKERS

# Violins

by Holly Saari

Watch the **bow** move smoothly up and down. See her fingers press on the strings. Hear the pretty sounds. Zin, zin, zin. She is playing the violin.

A girl plays the violin at a concert.

The violin is a **string instrument**. It has four strings. They help make the sounds.

A man plays the violin.

A violin's body is made of wood. The strings are made of metal.

Violin strings are pulled tight.

A violin is played by pulling a bow across the strings. A bow is made of horsehair that is pulled tight and connected to a stick.

Three bows lie on sheets of music.

A **violinist** rests the violin between the chin and the shoulder. One hand moves the bow across the strings.

The violin has a place to rest the chin.

The other hand presses the strings at the end of the violin. The violinist jiggles this hand on the string to make the sound move back and forth.

A violinist's hands are always moving.

People play different kinds of music on the violin. Two kinds of music are classical and country. A violin can also be plucked, like a guitar.

A violinist plays classical music.

Violins are important in an **orchestra**. An orchestra is a music group that has many instruments. Violins are the biggest **section** in an orchestra.

Violinists sit in the front of the orchestra.

Violins are about 500 years old. They were first played in Italy. Today they are played all around the world.

A man gets ready to play his violin in Morocco.

Zin, zin, zin. Playing the violin is so much fun!

A young violinist has fun practicing.

# Glossary

**bow (BOH):** A bow is the long stick that is pulled across a violin to make a sound. A violin player uses a bow.

**orchestra (OR-kess-truh):** An orchestra is a large group of people who play instruments together. An orchestra may have several violins in it.

**section (SEK-shun):** A section is a part of something larger. An orchestra has a violin section.

**string instrument (STRING IN-struh-munt):** A string instrument is an instrument that makes sound by pressing or plucking strings. The violin is a string instrument.

**violinist (vy-uh-LIN-ist):** A person who plays the violin is called a violinist. A violinist has to practice to be good.

# To Find Out More

## Books

Elliott, Katie. *The Fun Factory Violin Book*. London: Boosey & Hawkes, 2004.

Levine, Robert T. *The Story of the Orchestra*. New York: Black Dog & Leventhal Publishers, 2001.

Moss, Lloyd. *Zin! Zin! Zin! A Violin*. New York: Aladdin Paperbacks, 2005.

## Web Sites

Visit our Web site for links about violins: *childsworld.com/links*

Note to Parents, Teachers, and Librarians: We routinely verify our Web links to make sure they are safe and active sites. So encourage your readers to check them out!

# Index

# About the Author

**Holly Saari** enjoys contributing to children's education through the written word. She's an avid reader and also likes to practice playing the piano.

**On the cover: Fingers press on violin strings.**

Published by The Child's World®
1980 Lookout Drive • Mankato, MN 56003-1705
800-599-READ • www.childsworld.com

ACKNOWLEDGMENTS
The Child's World®: Mary Berendes, Publishing Director
The Design Lab: Design and production
Red Line Editorial: Editorial direction

PHOTO CREDITS: iStockphoto, cover, 9; Evgeniy Gorbunov/
iStockphoto, 3, 15; Svemir/Shutterstock, 5; Anne Kitzman/
Shutterstock, 7; Parker Deen/iStockphoto, 11; Bryce Newell/
iStockphoto, 13; MCale/Shutterstock, 17; Luis Ducoing/iStockphoto,
19; Yenwen Lu/iStockphoto, 21

Printed in the United States of America in Mankato, Minnesota.
November 2009
F11460

LIBRARY OF CONGRESS CATALOGING-IN-PUBLICATION DATA
Saari, Holly.
  Violins / by Holly Saari.
    p. cm. — (Music makers)
  Includes index.
  ISBN 978-1-60253-358-5 (library bound : alk. paper)
  1. Violin—Juvenile literature.  I. Title. II. Series.
  ML800.S23 2010
  787.2'19—dc22                      2009030210